REFLECTIONS IN THE SEASONS

Daniella M. Butler

Reflections in the Seasons
Daniella M. Butler

No part of this publication may be reproduced, distributed, or transmitted in any form or by any means, including photocopying, recording, or other electronic or mechanical methods, without the prior written permission of the publisher, except in the case of brief quotations embodied in critical reviews and certain other noncommercial uses permitted by copyright law. For permission requests, write to the author, addressed "Attention: Permissions " at info@daniellambutler.com.

Copyright © 2025 Daniella Butler Trust
All rights reserved.

Butler, Daniella M.
Reflections in the Seasons
www.DaniellaMButler.com
Email: info@daniellambutler.com

ISBN: 979-8-9921648-6-2 (Hardcover)

First Edition: June 21, 2025
Book Cover Art by: Kristina Cardoza

Printed in the United States of America

Contents

ALL SEASONS, 1

Seasons of Love, 3
Season's Cycle, 4
Love Through the Seasons, 5

All Seasons Quest, 6

WINTER, 9

Winter's Love, 11
Winter Holiday Season, 12
Winter's Rose, 13
Winter Forest Family, 14
Winter Humans, 15
Winter Solstice Love, 16
Polar Night Moon, 17
Winter Magic, 18
Winter Trees, 19
Winter Darkness, 20
Goodbye Winter, 21

Winter Quest, 22

SPRING, 25

First Spring Kill, 27
Spring Aurora Lights, 28
Spring Renewed, 29
Let's Talk About Spring, 30
Spring of Love, 31
Spring of the Robins, 32
Dawn of Spring, 33
Spring Equinox, 34
My Favorite is Spring, 35
Hello Spring, 36
Goodbye Spring, 37

Spring Quest, 38

SUMMER, 41

Hello Summer, 43
Summer Seeds, 44
Rainbow Cloud, 45
Reptile Summer, 46
The Salmon Call, 47
Summer Lightning, 48
Summer Firefly Life, 49

Summer Solstice Love, 50
Summer Creation, 51
Goodbye, Magical Summer Sky, 52
Summer's End, 53

Summer Quest, 54

AUTUMN, 57

Aurora Moon, 59
Autumn Love Story, 60
Autumn's First Love, 61
Farewell Autumn Love, 62
Planted Fall Love, 63
Autumn's Nature, 64
Celebrating Autumn, 65
Liquid Rainbow, 66
Autumn Daisy, 67
Falling Love, 68
Autumn's End, 69

Autumn Quest, 70

From the Author, 73

Reflections in the Seasons

ALL SEASONS

Seasons of Love

For the true love of me,
Me with a heart now free.
Free to love whomever I wish,
Wish indulged in seasons of bliss.

Bliss ignited by my heart's passion.
Passion once buried beneath the ashen.
Ashen that tightly entrapped one's heart,
Heart long enchanted by my love's first start.

Start with the spring-filled blooming wishes,
Wishes with the warmth of the summer kisses.
Kisses on autumn leaves blown to heart's places,
Places where true love grew from its winter traces.

Traces of love's footsteps within the seasons,
Seasons bring forth the playful past of treasons.
Treasons from childhood heart that's now forgiven,
Forgiven by true love's maturity that has finally risen.

Season's Cycle

Plant it
Before the last leaf falls.
Bury it
Beneath the autumn walls.
Cover it
Under the blanket of winter.
Hide it
In the cold, like a lonely spinster.
Sprout it
In the rain from the renewed Spring.
Nourish it
For the blooming flowers, it will bring.
Free it
In the bright sunshine of the summertime.
Birth it
Into the new seeds for our next lifetime.

Love Blossom Seeds Grow

Wishing you season's well
Through all of nature's spells.
Beautiful rose behold;
Her secrets now be told.

Wish on raining white snow
Where falling leaves once blow.
The warmth of seeds she brings
Once bloomed by pollen wings.

Blessings from a prayer
Sent to season's players.
My love starts with a seed
Grows like blossoming weeds.

Love you through the seasons.
Love you for good reasons.
In this life and beyond,
Linked by nature's bond.

All Seasons Quest

1. What's your favorite season and why?
2. If you could get rid of one season, which one would it be?
3. Now write a short poem about questions 1 and 2.

Your turn to write...

Winter

Winter's Love

Heart whispering wish,
Wish upon a snowflake kiss.
Kiss that warmed the iciest cold,
Cold that shivered within my soul.

Soul renewed in clarity of love,
Love on the wings of a flying dove.
Dove that remained without migration,
Migration meant leaving true love's station.

Station me in a place where I contrast the white,
White canvas allows me to be a vision in your sight.
Sight brings clear foresight for your eyes to being told,
Told of love waiting for you in the harshness of the cold.

Winter Holiday Season

Snow is falling
From the heavens above.
Winter is bawling
From the happiness of love.

Holiday wish
Of the tear-filled snow
Brings a backdrop of cheer
For family's smiling faces to glow.

Though winter
Brings a dangerous drive,
Distance will still enter
Toward a lover's shrive.

For it is that time
Of gathering relatives near.
A family's winter chime
At this merry time of the year.

Winter's Rose

Cold moon
In chill of night.
Seed beneath frost
Is hidden from sight.

The sprouting soul
Of Lenten rose.
Growth blooming
In winter's pose.

Painted beauty
On canvas white.
Blossoming in trials
Towards love's light.

Elegant contrast
Of this rose of winter.
Harshness cannot deny
This majestic stinter.

Winter Forest Family

I'm in love with my forest prince;
He keeps me warm in winter's wince.
With danger lurking all around,
He keeps our family safe and sound.

There'll be a time when he's no more;
My son must rise and take his ore.
He follows his father's snow trace,
To lead us to a new safe space.

Nature is beautiful and cruel,
None crueler than facing men's duel.
For now, I watch the winter race;
In my arms, my family's embrace.

Winter Humans

Winter wonderland
Type of run.
All the humans
Are having fun.

Slide together
Go down the slope.
Winter season
Renewing hope.

Nature gave humans
No fur cloak.
So, whose fur is it
On that bloke!

Winter humans
Are having fun.
They're so cute
When they have no guns.

Winter Solstice Love

I met you
On the shortest daylight
Of the year.
One Winter Solstice,
December 21.

The Earth tilted
At our first meeting.
As the sun greeted us,
Moving in closer
From up high.

So, each winter
I'm reminded
Of the first day
That I met
My winter solstice love.

Polar Night Moon

Winter darkness,
I'm never alone,
The polar night moon
Will guide me home.

In this dark place
Where there's no sunlight,
My love will always
Shine in day night.

Winter darkness
May last a season;
My love for you
Will only deepen.

My heart now tells
The soul moon goodbye.
I'll miss you
Till our next lunar sky.

Winter Magic

Winter lovers followed path seeks
A magical place where the cold peaks.

Snow squalls paint the Earth white;
Filling the ground with its winter sight.
Wood frogs are frozen within their place;
Patiently waiting for the next season's grace.
Frost quakes boomed loudly under the ground,
Gaining attention to its crackling, peculiar sound.

Frozen bubbles of methane gas;
This glittering beauty of jewelry mass.
Frost flowers in her alluringness of swirls;
Beautiful pattern that seeps as plants' pearls.
Stoats change their fur coat to the snow's white
In an inauguration prepared for the winter's light.

Magic happens in a place of scarce sun;
So, lovers can enjoy the chill of winter fun.

The Winter Trees

Icicle hanging on the winter trees,
Decorated stiffly against hail breeze.
Frozen water of the winter sprites;
Meticulously formed in crystal lights.

Magical snowflakes falling from the sky,
Each with a unique pattern from up high.
Delicately resting on the evergreen trees,
Winter decorations this season's freeze.

Pretty is the bloom of the wintersweet;
Contrasting against the drops of sleet.
Nature's decoration on canvas white,
Another winter tree for season's delight.

Decorated brights of winter fireflies,
Streaming across trees despite the bise.
This is the season of the winter trees,
So, nature adorned its own with ease.

Winter Darkness

Dark is the night
Of the winter moon.
Deep are the stars
That shine bright up above.
So, I'm not alone
Cause you're always there.

Day remains night
In the polar moon.
Season hides sun
From the sky up above.
But I'm not alone
Cause you're always near.

Darkness turns light
When the seasons change.
I must be brave
And wait for the dawn.
Cause I'm not alone
You were always here.

Goodbye Winter

Melting away the winter's trace,
And saying goodbye to my chilly face.
No more sledding down mountain space,
For the next season is taking winter's place.

Removing white from the winter stoat,
For all are putting away their winter coat.
Setting aside the carols from the songs I wrote,
Sailing away on the melted lake of spring's boat.

Winter Quest

1. What do you do during the winter months?
2. What thought comes to mind when you think of winter?
3. Now write a short poem about the first two questions.

Your turn to write...

Spring

First Spring Kiss

Spring gifts me
A kind of bliss,
Bliss formed
From my first love's kiss.

Kiss upon
An open bud;
Bud blossoming
Far from mud.

Mud footsteps
On lover's trail.
Trail to curtain
Creepers' veil.

Veil hid
Pieces of my soul.
Soul carrying heart
Now whole.

Spring Aurora Light

The beautiful aurora dances
On a night spring lake in the sky.
Her celestial brush stroke is painted
In living movements twirling up high.

On the night frozen lake of the heavens,
Backdrop in darkness of the starry sky,
Aurora's majestic Swan Lake dance
Is performed on a stage up high.

With Aurora in emerald green
Racing across spring canvas night,
Pink, red, blue, and purple are all seen
Hypnotizing admirers in a colorful flight.

Transcending of the aurora to the heavens
Of the darkest of the night in the spring,
As it lights up the night like flames
Dancing across the sky as it sings.

Spring Renewed

Pitapat, pitapat
Spring rain shower.
Sadness cleansed
At an audacious hour.

Worm-filled loosening
Of the hardened dirt,
Causes a rebirth to bloom
As love rises from the Earth.

Pitapat, pitapat
Spring rain shower.
Sadness released
At the perfect hour.

Loving you
Is the easiest thing to do.
For each spring
Our love's rebirth is due.

Let's Talk About Spring

Let's sing about the birds
And the butterflies.
Let's look at the beauty
Of spring's rise.
Let's spring in the air
Like we don't care.
Let's soak in the warmth
For spring is here.

Hmm, magic, magic spring,
You cause my heart to sing.

Let's talk about the bees
And the flower sight.
Let's watch Spring's baby
Birds first flight.
Let's smile at the bears
Awake spring stares.
Let's all now be happy
Cause spring is here.

Spring of Love

The beauty of spring
Can make the heart sing.
Blossoming passion of love,
Seems to shine down from above.

Each bud is like a love story,
One filled with battles of glory.
As a pedal falls down to the ground,
Two swords cling a passionate sound.

The shower of raindrops
Wash the past from mountaintops.
Now renewed from the past heartache
To peacefully relaxing on the spring lake.

Spring of the Robins

Way up high nestled in the tree,
Where the birds built a nest to be,
Two robins take a daring flight,
Singing as one in spring's sunlight.

For spring is renewal this year;
Saying goodbye to winter's smear.
Now robins can fulfill their quest,
Laying blue eggs in empty nests.

Baby robins hatch from their shells,
In their parents' hearts they now dwell.
Nature's instincts will always win,
When life's new creations begin.

Parent robins work together.
Babies grow big with more feathers.
It's time to tell their nest goodbye,
And learn to soar up in the sky.

Dawn of Spring

In the dawning
Of the season spring,
The birds grow brighter,
Then mates will sing.

Pretty cherry blossoms
Blooms in light.
Magnolias cast
A pageant sight.

Alluring smells
Of the season spring,
Colorful vision,
A sight it brings.

Splashes of color
On Mother Earth,
For it's the season
Of renewed birth.

Spring Equinox

Day and night,
Equal sides to one.
First day
Of spring equinox.

My yin to your yang
Becomes one,
As sun shines
On the equator.

Bloom in light
Of spring equinox,
In illume
Of the equator.

For this is the first
Day of Spring
All equal
In births of nature.

My Favorite is Spring

Mother Nature, build me wings
To fly up high to see spring.
Like an eagle soaring high,
I see beauty from the sky.

Give me a year filled with spring,
Not that frost that winter brings.
No hot heat from summer sun,
Or dead leaves during fall's run.

Spring is the best time of year,
When love is blooming, my dear.
Other seasons can't compare,
Spring will always win each year.

In a place where spring won't end,
That's where you'll find me, my friend.
Fragrant smells of spring flowers,
Surround me this spring hour.

Hello Spring

Daffodils bloom
At the first sight of spring.
Robins fly back
In the warmth with happy wings.
Frogs spawn
A new beginning with their egg rings.
Bees pollinate
In all the colors while buzzing as they sing.
Hibernation stops
For the warmth provides more food to bring.
Human children
Go outside in the spring to play on their swings.
Hello to you,
Welcome, my colorful first day of the season spring.

Goodbye Spring

Warmer heat
Means the summer is pending.
Peonies hideaway
As spring approaches its near ending.
Warblers say goodbye
At sight of spring's downward descending.
Butterflies emerge
In a colorful sight in their upward ascending.
And more bugs
Come to play for next season they are attending.
Goodbye,
For now, the magic of season spring is now ending.

Spring's Talks

1. What is your favorite thing that happens during spring?
2. What thought comes to mind when you think of spring?
3. Now write a short poem about the first two questions.

Your turn to write...

Summer

Hello Summer

Hello summer
With heated sun,
Sun like the Arctic
Full day fun.
Fun with kites
Below cotton clouds.
Clouds above
The festival crowds.

Crowds can enjoy
Heat of the night.
Night where meteors
Hit the ground.
Ground tattooed
With universe marks.
Marks the beauty
Of summer sparks.

Summer Seeds

Annual reign
Of summer's love
Seeds produced from kisses
Then sprinkled from hearts above.

One of nature's creations
Created in the summer season.
A token for upcoming generations
Produced in the sunshine of life's reason.

For seeds are the hearts
Of nature's love's beginning.
Summer is the season's first start
To the previous season's upbringings.

A small, encoded seed
Produced in the summertime,
Can become a massive tree when freed
To grow in the boundaries of nature's prime.

Rainbow Cloud

Pretty rainbow cloud,
Painted pastel cotton candy
In the days of the summer sky.

Like a coloring book,
Coloring in pencil on clouds
Etched in days of the summer sun.

This picturesque beauty
Painted by nature's brush
In warmth of the summer sky.

Like a painting up high,
A surreal, magical cloud mist
Painted in heat of the summer sun.

Reptile Summer

Happy is the reptile's eye,
Basking in summer heat sky.
Gaze like sun with yellow stare;
Warm him up in summer's air.

Keeping all the bugs at bay;
Summer most come out to play.
Bugs play an essential role,
Then eaten by reptiles whole.

Content with the summer bliss,
Some creatures on Spirit's list.
Playing in warmth of the sun,
Reptile's time of summer fun.

The Salmon Call

Nature is calling me
To come home,
Upstream to a place
Where I was born.
A dangerous river swim
I accept,
For I am mesmerized
With her calls.

We migrate
In spite of the danger,
And some of us
Will meet our maker.
But those of us
Who made it home safe,
Next generation
Spawns in our place.

Summer Lightning

Hide me away
From the thunder and lightning,
Who causes summer to seem frightening.

Hide all the stars
From the lightning in the dark up high,
With roots sketched across the summer sky.

Hide all the trees
From being stuck by this Titan,
In the wildfire days of summer lightning.

Hide me under covers
Of a childhood thunderous rainy night.
All grown up to this uncanny summer sight.

Summer Firefly Life

In the summer mountains
Way up high,
Synchronizing fireflies
Take to the sky.

Two years as larvae
That's bound to the ground,
Freedom is the night sky
Where mates are found.

Males sync dazzling lights
To draw mates near,
Mates will shine back
When nature's love is clear.

With less than a month
To firefly tomb,
She quickly lays many eggs
From her womb.

Summer Solstice Love

I met you
On the longest day
Of the year.
One Summer Solstice,
June 21.

The Earth tilted
At our first meeting.
The sun salutes us
At the highest
Position in the sky.

So, each summer
I'm reminded
Of the first day,
When I met
My summer solstice love.

Summer Creation

Summer is that time
Of the year,
When your warmth
Is felt through the air.

Like supermoon
Close to the Earth,
Magic happens
During summer births.

As meteors
Fall to the ground,
Love's night backdrop
Is found.

For the season to mate
Is clear,
Summer baby making
Is here.

Goodbye, Magical Summer Sky

I set sail on a summer breeze,
Putting my soul at temporary ease.
Visiting Arctic Circle for summer play
Where Midnight Sun shines the entire day.
Now onward to look at pretty rainbow clouds,
Far away, from sun-worshipping beach crowds.

Night waterfall skies birth a magical moonbow,
A beautiful pixie dust called a lunar rainbow.
Baby turtles walk the beach of the night sky
To the water beneath the moon up high.
Time to sail back on a summer breeze,
For my soul is content and at ease.

This season's brilliant summer's ray,
A precarious time that beckons me to stay,
But alas, it's time to say my summer goodbye.
So, goodbye for now, to my magical summer sky.

Summer's End

Enriched greenery
Of my summer throne.
Threatened by next season
In her crimson and amber tones.
Elegant is the green
Of the fresh-cut smell of grass.
A smell that holds memories
Of my playful, youthful past.
My summer love
Dressed for heartfelt warm weather.
Childhood days
Of searching for buried treasure.
The sun is blazing brightly
In the height of the clear blue sky,
And kites are rising
Upward to meet her up high.
Goodbye, goodbye summer
For autumn is calling.
My foliage summer love
Created seeds that are now falling.

Summer Quest

1. What's your favorite summer memory?
2. What thought comes to mind when you think of summer?
3. Now write a short poem about the first two questions.

Your turn to write...

Autumn

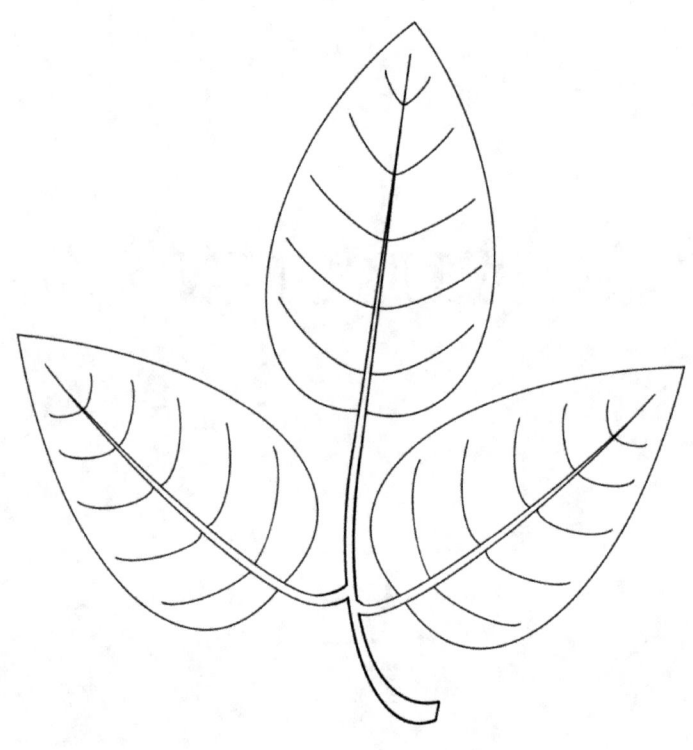

Aurora Moon

Alluring orange
Of the Harvest Moon,
Moon of autumn
In mysterious rune.
Rune of the exquisite
Aurora light,
Light so celestial
Beyond eyes' sight.

Sight of pretty angels
Dancing in sky,
Sky filled with the aurora
Upwards high.
High is the night canvas
Of her beauty,
Beauty beholds
Harvest Moon's love duty.

Autumn Love Story

Day and night mutual love,
Entwined in autumn equinox.
Fear migration of runaway dove,
The hiding feelings of autumn fox.

Harvest Moon sings of our love story,
Playing in leaves fallen from trees high.
Moonlit walks speak of the season's glory,
As beautiful aurora romances the night sky.

Autumn love last seasons beyond this year,
With pumpkin patch kisses from my love.
Autumn is the season for love my dear,
A gift of matrimony from stars above.

Autumn's First Love

Autumn pigment
Of a colorful scenic Earth.
Leaves are falling
On a painted canvas dirt.
A picturesque place
For my heartfelt first spurt.
Decorative holiday
Of autumn love's dessert.

Never leave me
During the migration alert.
My dear, I love you
Through all of fall's hurt.
Confession of love
To my autumn heart flirt.
My amber beauty
Now keeps our love peart.

Farewell Autumn Love

As the leaf begins to fall,
It glides firm against wind's call;
Downward into its beginning.

As it lays upon Earth's chest,
It completes its nature's quest;
Memories of past reconnecting.

As it sinks into dirt's start,
Now it's pieces of Earth's heart;
Happy when hearing your singing.

Farewell, farewell, my autumn love.
Renew, renew from tears above.
See you at fall's rebeginning.

Planted Fall Love

Fall together and let's all sing
Of the beauty that autumn brings.
Seeds are planted inside the dirt
Nourished by leaf falls upon the Earth.

Fall's the seasonal time of year
That transitional births appear.
Colorful is the nature's scene
Then her autumn becomes unseen.

Fall together and let's all sing
Of the magic our autumn brings.
Seeds are buried beneath the ground
Covered in leaf falls in a mound.

Painted, painted my autumn leaves.
Beauty, beauty, my love retrieves.
First trimester of planted seeds,
Beneath the ground, my love now breeds.

Autumn's Nature

The monarch butterflies take flight
To warmer places when cold is in sight,
For autumn is that magic time of year
To migrate when winter season is near.

Thicker furs grow on my furry friends,
Mother Nature's gift coat till winter ends,
For autumn means time for preparation;
No extra furs fall to hibernation.

Chickadees' brains grow to a larger size,
For autumn is the season to grow wise.
Gather, then store food for the occasion
Are the goals of those with no migration.

Sun makes the equator's night and day stall,
For autumn equinox marks start of fall.
Animals' moods shift in fall equinox;
Nature's connection of internal clocks.

Celebrating Autumn

Harvest grows on fall-autumn vine.
Propitious moon from the divine
The yellow, orange, red, and brown
Of autumn festivals in town.

Children wearing Hallow's costumes,
Dressed in plastics, metals, and plumes.
Candy eating with pumpkin pie,
Orange moon in Aurora's sky.

The celestial stars of autumn
Family gathering custom.
Colorful leaves fall to the ground,
To say goodbye to autumn's bound.

Liquid Rainbow

Crimson river
In her pink to red tones,
Autumn blossoming
On her river stones.

The river plant
Blooms in stunning bright red,
And align the floors
Of the riverbed.

Colorful
Blue, yellow, orange, and green,
May also debut
In this autumn scene.

The liquid rainbow,
An impressive sight,
Will come alive
In autumn fall's sunlight.

Autumn Daisy

Montauk daisy,
Fall is here,
So, my beauty,
Don't despair.

Stay with me
Until the frost.
Never fear
The winter's rost.

Winter
Ends your curtain call,
Stay within
My autumn fall.

If you choose
To disappear,
Come back to me
Fall next year.

Falling Love

My love won't die
Even when your leaves fall,
For your beauty remains
Inside your hall.

My love won't wither
Like leaves on the ground.
For leaves will grow back
In the seasons' bound.

My love won't end
When leaves fall, my dear.
For my love renews
Throughout every year.

My love won't die
In your changing seasons,
For true love will endure
Nature's reasons.

Autumn's End

Leaves are falling,
Autumn is stalling.
Fall, but I held tight
With my entire might.

Must stay much longer,
And grow a little stronger.
Winter is trying to take my place,
Removing the pieces, leaving no trace.

Put back the color of my painted autumn tones,
I must resist the next chapter that will chill my bones.
But love says it will love me in the chapters of each season,
To have faith, move forward, and trust in love as the reason.

And so, I must say goodbye, for my season is now ending,
Imprint me in your heart after autumn's transcending.

Autumn Quest

1. What do you look forward to doing during the fall season?
2. What thought comes to mind when you think of autumn?
3. Now write a short poem about the first two questions.

Your turn to write...

From the Author

Hi, I'm Daniella M. Butler, the author of this book. These poems and songs were inspired by the reflection of life and nature within each season. I hope you enjoyed reading them as much as I enjoyed writing them.

This book was written early because my daughter liked the "For the Love of Me" section of my poetry book, *In Her Skin: The Black Woman*, and asked me to write more about love. I already had plans to write this book, so I incorporated a few love poems. The book also took on a life of its own.

Let's talk about autumn. Because of the love of poetry, autumn changed to fall in North America. The word autumn is used formally. Flowers spring up and leaves fall down. Makes sense. It also helps when changing the clock during daylight saving time—spring forward in spring and fall back in fall. I used autumn purely because it sounds pretty to me. Thank you.

Follow me at @daniellambutler on Amazon, YouTube, IG, Rumble, BlueSky, Threads, Pinterest, FanBase, X and more. GoodReads: @daniellabutler. Facebook: @daniellambutlerauthor

www.ingramcontent.com/pod-product-compliance
Lightning Source LLC
Chambersburg PA
CBHW050523100526
44581CB00002B/94